YOR
Gho

Prepare to be frightened by these terrifying tales
from around Yorkshire

By

Richard Holland

BRADWELL
BOOKS

Published by Bradwell Books
9 Orgreave Close Sheffield S13 9NP
Email: books@bradwellbooks.co.uk
©Richard Holland 2014

British Library Cataloguing in Publication Data: a catalogue
record for this book is available from the British Library.

1st Edition
ISBN: 9781909914049

Print: Gomer Press, Llandysul, Ceredigion SA44 4JL
Design by: jenksdesign@yahoo.co.uk
Photograph Credits: ShutterStock and Richard Holland

CONTENTS

Whitby Abbey is one of Yorkshire's best-known haunted places
Shutterstock/Deborah Benbrook

INTRODUCTION

Yorkshire is – or rather was – England's largest county. So great an area does it cover, however, that in the 20th century it was carved up into four distinct counties: North Yorkshire, South Yorkshire, East (or the East Riding of) Yorkshire and West (or the West Riding of) Yorkshire. The county is rich in history, boasting some of the finest castles and religious buildings (ruinous or gloriously preserved) anywhere in Britain. The House of York was, of course, one side of the 15th-century War of the Roses, fought against noblemen of the House of Lancaster (whose symbol was the red rose, while York's was the white). Yorkshire also had a key role in the English Civil War and became one of the powerhouses of the Industrial Revolution. Its fertile farmland and wool production made it one of the wealthiest counties in England, from the early Middle Ages onwards.

Today millions visit Yorkshire to enjoy its glorious countryside, which includes two National Parks: the Yorkshire Dales and the North York Moors. With such a vast landmass and so much history, the old county of Yorkshire certainly had a right to lay claim to being the most haunted in the British Isles. York was the first to market itself to tourists as Britain's most haunted city (others have since tried to claim the crown) and Whitby enjoys particular favour with fans of the Gothic.

But York and Whitby are by no means the only haunted towns in Yorkshire: Leeds, Sheffield, Bradford and Hull are just a few which can boast a host of ghosts. Then there are the county's many beautiful stately homes and those aforementioned castles and abbeys, many possessed of their own particular phantom or phantoms. Even the wild open spaces are not immune from paranormal activity and more than a few travellers have encountered ghosts on Yorkshire's roads.

Whether you're lucky enough to be a Yorkshire resident or one of its very many enthusiastic visitors, an exploration of its haunted heritage may yield a better chance of seeing a ghost than any other county in England.

Fountains Abbey, near Ripon, is just one Yorkshire's many beautiful and impressive haunted locations.
Shutterstock/chris2766

THE GHOSTS OF YORK

The ancient city of York is one of the most visited in Britain.
Every year hordes of tourists from the UK and abroad
descend on the city, attracted by its great beauty and
extraordinary heritage. There was a small Celtic settlement
here when the Romans arrived. In AD 71 the Romans began
to build a mighty fortress in its place and they named it
Eboracum. By the Middle Ages, long after the Romans had
left, Eboracum had grown into a major town and trading
centre. For many years it was at the heart of the Danelaw,
that portion of northern England controlled by the Vikings.
The Norsemen named it Jorvik.

A great deal has survived of medieval York, from its
magnificent Minster to the delightfully wonky architecture
of timber-framed houses which can be found crammed into
narrow streets such as the Shambles. A section of the Roman
defensive wall survives in Museum Street and Viking York is
preserved in the Jorvik Centre museum. It would be a
surprise indeed if a place so steeped in history did not boast
more than a few ghosts and York is indeed famous for its
hauntings.

Let us begin with arguably the best-known ghost sighting in
the city and one which features perhaps York's oldest spooks.
In 1953 assistant plumber Harry Martindale was working
alone in the cellar of Treasurer's House in Chapter House
Street near the Minster. It was cold and quiet down there
and the last thing Mr Martindale expected to hear was the
blast of a horn or trumpet. Mr Martindale turned in the
direction of the sound, wondering where it could have come

York is a city with a rich heritage and the ghosts to match.
Shutterstock/Mauro Bighin

from. How, he wondered, could it have penetrated through the thick walls all that way below the level of the street? He was still puzzling over this when he got a bigger surprise.

Suddenly, a Roman soldier on horseback rode proudly through the wall. He was followed by a company of foot-soldiers, each armed with short-bladed swords or lances and each wearing the distinctively Roman style of armour and helmet. They marched two-abreast past the astonished Mr Martindale, of whom they took no notice whatsoever. The ghostly legionnaires were clearly walking on a level even lower than that of the cellar, for their knees disappeared down into the stone floor. After the roaming Romans had passed through into the opposite wall, the frightened plumber scrambled out of the cellar and told the curator what he had seen. This sensible man encouraged Mr Martindale to write down his experience as a permanent record. Thanks to this, it has become a classic of English ghost-lore.

Archaeological investigation has since uncovered a Roman military station near Treasurer's House and a road of the same period passing directly beneath it, at about the level described by Mr Martindale (successive building over the centuries has, of course, elevated modern York several yards above its earliest habitation). Treasurer's House is open to the public and is in the care of the National Trust, which describes it as an 'elegant town house dating from medieval times'.

Mr Martindale's ghost sighting was not the only one recorded in York in 1953. That same year the caretaker of

Treasurer's House is the scene of arguably York's most famous ghost sighting.
National Trust Images/Nick Meers

the Yorkshire Museum made headlines after he announced that he had encountered a man in Edwardian clothing in the library. He told the press:

'He looked as a solid as you or I and I thought he was a real person. He was dressed in a frock coat with drainpipe trousers and was wearing elastic-sided boots. I noticed that distinctly as there were no turn-ups to his trousers. He looked agitated and kept muttering to himself: "I must find it." He went to the bookshelf and started to rummage among the volumes. He seemed anxious to find something. I thought things had gone far enough, so thinking he must be deaf I reached out to touch his shoulder, and as I touched him he vanished.'

A few weeks later a book was found to have fallen from the shelf just where the ghost had been standing when it vanished. Inside the book was a note showing it had been donated to the library by one Alderman Edward Wooler, who had died in the 1920s. When a photograph of Alderman Wooler was obtained, the caretaker immediately recognised it as the ghost.

In the grounds of the museum are the ruins of the church which formerly belonged to the medieval Abbey of St Mary's. A phantom monk has frequently been glimpsed among the ruins. The Abbey belonged to the Benedictine order, whose members wore black robes. So too does the ghost, who has become known as 'the Black Abbot' over the years.

Another survivor of St Mary's Abbey is King's Manor, which dates back to the 15th century but stands on the site of an even earlier building used to house the abbots. It belongs to the University of York. In his book *Haunted York*, Rupert Matthews describes King's Manor as 'probably the most haunted building' in the city. One of its ghosts is that of a monk in a black habit. He may be the same ghost as that haunting the ruined church or one of the other hundreds of anonymous men who devoted their life to God during the long life of the abbey.

The ruins of St Mary's Abbey are in the grounds of the Yorkshire Museum.
Both buildings are haunted.
Shutterstock/WH CHOW

The best-known ghost of King's Manor, however, is that of a woman in a green gown. She is said to be slim and dark-haired and to be seen carrying a bunch of roses. Sometimes the swishing sound of her heavy skirts is heard. Tradition states that this is Anne Boleyn, who briefly stayed here with King Henry VIII while he was on one of his periodic journeys round his kingdom. Why Anne should haunt the house is not explained, however.

The staircase in the north wing is haunted by a man believed to be Sir Henry Hastings, who ordered the staircase to be built and who lived at King's Manor during the latter half of the 17th century. A peculiar phenomenon which took place for a number of years (although it has not been reported recently) has been linked to Sir Henry. On numerous occasions, a painting of an unidentified man of the same period as Sir Henry was found to have been lifted off the wall during the night and placed gently on the floor. Sir Henry's ghost was considered the most likely culprit, leading to the supposition that perhaps the man in the portrait is of none other than Sir Henry himself.

Finally, the courtyard at King's Manor is said to be haunted by not one but many ghosts, those of soldiers dating from the years of the English Civil War. These are the spirits of hundreds of wounded Parliamentarians who were crowded into the courtyard when it became a makeshift hospital. Sadly most of them died of their injuries or subsequent infection.

York's most striking medieval landmark is undoubtedly its Minster. 'Minster' is an Anglo-Saxon word referring to a missionary church, and recalls pagan Viking Jorvik. Its formal title is The Cathedral and Metropolitical Church of St Peter in York and it is the seat of the Archbishop of York. A church has been on the site since the 7th century but the glorious edifice we see today dates almost entirely from the 13th to the 15th centuries. The Minster was completed in 1472.

A number of ghosts have been reported at York Minster. The apparition of a man in Elizabethan costume, for example, has been seen sauntering in the nave. Equally anonymous are the two female figures glimpsed from time to time in the north transept. A clue to their identity is suggested by the fact that they manifest near a window dedicated to nurses

Ancient King's Manor is described by one researcher as 'probably the most haunted building in all of York'.
Shutterstock/ Alastair Wallace

who cared for the wounded during the First World War. More recognisable is the ghost of a notable clergyman, Dean Gale, who died in 1702. He has sometimes been seen sitting in the choir, gazing up at the pulpit. His first appearance was a few weeks after his decease, when the man appointed to succeed him was reading his debut service at Holy Communion. The new dean looked down to see his predecessor staring back at him! He froze with the shock and had to be helped out of the pulpit.

The other ghost said to have been seen on more than one occasion in the Minster is of a man who could not have been more different to the amiable Dean Gale. Jonathan Martin, born in 1783, was a religious fanatic whose obsessions became more and more extreme and potentially dangerous as the years progressed. It seems likely he was suffering from some form of progressive mental illness, or possibly brain damage brought on by a head wound he received when he served in the Royal Navy fighting the French. The unfortunate Martin spent time in an asylum and his time out of it writing threatening letters to clergymen he believed were in league with the devil.

His madness came to a head on 1 February 1829, when he concealed himself in the Minster until the visitors and clergy had left and it was locked up for the night. Martin then emerged from his hiding place, stripped himself naked and proceeded to bash up the furniture, which he piled up to form a pyre. He then set light to his holy bonfire and escaped through a smashed window as the flames took hold in the choir. The conflagration raged all night and was only put out the following morning, by which time it had done considerable damage to the medieval interior of the choir and other parts of the Minster.

At his trial, Martin made no attempt to deny his crime, but rather gloried in it, claiming that God had commanded him to start the fire in order to cleanse York of its sins. He was carted back off to the asylum, his belief that he was God's representative on Earth unshaken for the rest of his life. From time to time, it is said, Martin's ghost appears in the choir, but you may wish to avert your eyes if you do see this startling apparition, for Martin appears stark naked and capering about in mad glee.

Another spooky phenomenon linked with the Minster fire of 1829 is a mysterious blue light that drifts from the nave to the crossing. It is the size of a man. It was first spotted by a night watchman appointed shortly after Martin's escapade and it terrified the fierce dog he had with him. Of course, it's possible the pillar of light may have manifested on previous nights but formerly there had been no one around to witness it.

Finally, there is the amusing story of a woman who in the 1960s was standing outside the West Front of the Minster, watching restoration being carried out on the medieval stonework. The visitor's attention was drawn to one particularly fine carving up on the wall. As she was admiring it, she heard a man's voice beside her and she turned to see a little man in a scruffy gown with a shapeless sort of cap on his head. 'Do you like it?' he asked, indicating the carving. 'I did that!' Then he vanished.

A much more modest medieval church in the city, Holy Trinity in Micklegate, also has a haunted reputation. Here, in the 19th century, a parade of ghostly female figures, nicknamed 'the mother, the nursemaid and the child', would regularly be seen by worshippers and Sunday school children to pass by the east window. The figures' white robes were apparent behind the stained glass and the remaining details sharply distinct in the areas of clear glass. The group was described as 'seeming to enact a play beyond the glass' (to quote Jack Hallam's *Ghosts of the North*), the two taller figures apparently showing grief and distress over the head of the smaller 'child'. Their actions were not identical on each appearance, however. One witness recalled:

'On one occasion, when the mother and child had taken their departure, the medium figure – the nurse – waved her hands, and after walking slowly to the very edge of the window, turned round while on the pane of unstained glass, and waved her arm towards the other with what one would call a stage gesture, and then I most distinctly saw … the arm, bare nearly to the shoulder, with beautiful folds of white drapery hanging from it. Nothing could be plainer than the drag of the robes on the ground after the figures as they retired at the edge of the window where the clear glass was.'

Such detail implies more than a mere optical illusion and no explanation has been offered as to how such an elaborate

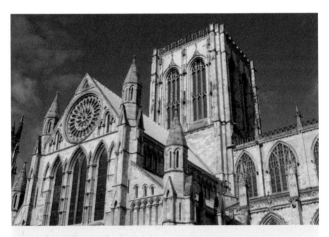

Several ghosts have been reported at the magnificent York Minster.
Shutterstock/northallertonman

effect might have been created. The phenomenon remains enigmatic, with explanations being offered from 'mass hallucination' to ghosts of plague victims or nuns from a priory which used to occupy the site. Holy Trinity was largely remodelled later in the 19th century and the women in white have not been seen since.

Although the identity of the Holy Trinity apparitions as nuns is conjectural, there seems no doubt in regards to another of York's celebrated ghosts, the 'Grey Lady'. The Grey Lady's haunt is an unusual one for a nun, however: the Theatre Royal. The explanation for this is that she dates back to the 15th century when a hospital stood on the ground now occupied by the St Leonard's Place theatre. Her story is a tragic one but somewhat standard for ghostly nuns, that she was walled up alive for committing an 'unpardonable sin', probably of having the misfortune to fall in love. The Grey Lady has most often been encountered in a dressing room but an actress got a clear view of her grey robes and white coif as she peered out of a stage box.

The Theatre Royal is also said to be haunted by an amorous actor of the 18th century. He fought and lost a duel with a rival for the attentions of a chorus girl. Death failed to prevent him from 'going on with the show', however, for his ghost was seen to stride boldly onto the stage during a performance of his latest play, much to the horror of his understudy. Although this was to be the actor's last time treading the boards, his ghost has continued to haunt the theatre for many years.

Mysterious white figures were regularly seen by scores of people at Holy Trinity Church during the mid-19th century.
Shutterstock/Petrafler

Several of York's impressive medieval bridges have survived. One of these, the Bootham Bar, is haunted by an anonymous nun. The name of the sad spectre haunting the environs of the Micklegate Bar is known to us, however. She is Sarah Brocklebank, whose father was kicked out of his job as gatekeeper when the key to the Micklegate went missing. He lost his position and they both lost their home. Sarah's father was convinced the loss was her fault and she spent the rest of her life trying to prove him wrong, going so far as to pick over the city's rubbish tips in search of the key. In the end her obsession with finding the missing key turned into madness and her deranged spirit is still said to be searching for it.

A number of other, less impressive buildings in York also have their ghosts. An old house in Goodramgate, for example, is haunted by a crippled boy called Marmaduke Buckle, who hanged himself in misery at his disability at the age of seventeen. In an upstairs room, there was found scored into the plaster the following legend: 'Marmaduke Buckle 1697–1715', with the number '17' scratched beneath. His little ghost has been glimpsed on the stairs and his invisible presence has been known to play pranks, such as switching the lights on and off.

Another child haunted No. 5 College Street. In the 1930s the then owners told how they would hear the voice of a child calling from a bedroom and sometimes hear it sobbing. It was seen just once: the apparition of a little girl skipping up the stairs. The family called in a medium, who claimed to have made contact with the girl and then related a tragic circumstance in which the child became the only survivor of

York's Theatre Royal, haunted by an actor and, more incongruously, a nun.
Shutterstock/Alastair Wallace

the plague when it descended on the house in the 17th century. The house was quarantined and locked up. One by one all the family members and servants died, leaving the little girl alone and afraid in a house of death, until she too succumbed to the disease. This chilling story could not, of course, be substantiated.

Among the many haunted pubs and hotels in York can be counted the Dean Court Hotel (haunted by a humble cleaner); the Punch Bowl (by a former landlord); the Windmill (by the ghost of an ostler); the Golden Fleece (by a Canadian air force officer); the Cock & Bottle (haunted by various ghosts, including one thought to be of George Villiers, the Duke of Buckingham); and the Black Swan (where the legs of a man – but only his legs – have been seen descending a staircase).

Shambles, or The Shambles as visitors generally call it, is one of York's most popular tourist destinations, a narrow bustling street of overhanging, timber-framed medieval houses, most of which have now been converted into shops, cafés and other attractions. One of these ancient edifices is known as 'the Pearl of York' and it contains a shrine to a woman who was canonised by the Pope as late as 1970. St Margaret Clitherow had lived in the house during the reign of Elizabeth I. She was a Catholic, a risky thing to be at the time, and she significantly increased the risk to her life and liberty by creating a secret chamber in her home in order to hide visiting priests. With numerous plots abroad to depose and murder the Protestant Queen, harbouring priests was a serious offence.

At length, Margaret was caught but she refused to admit to something she considered to be no crime and refused to plead either guilty or not guilty. This left the court with no choice but to extract a confession, or at least her co-operation, through a torture known as 'pressing'. They laid a board over the unfortunate Margaret, onto which they placed heavy weights, one at a time. Her spirit remained uncrushed but her body gave way, and Margaret died. She believed she was dying for her faith and refused to her last breath to acknowledge any wrongdoing. A shrine to St Margaret can now be visited in her former home. The house is haunted by a vague apparition, that of a woman – inevitably this has been linked to St Margaret Clitherow, and many believe it to be the visiting spirit of this brave martyr.

In 2010, ghost-hunter Darren Ritson wrote a report for *Paranormal Magazine* (of which I was then editor) on an investigation at two properties in Shambles carried out by the Ghost and Hauntings Overnight Surveillance Team (G.H.O.S.T.). Darren and G.H.O.S.T. held overnight vigils in Nos 22 and 44, Shambles, both owned by a Mr Simon Cox, who runs gift shops in each of them.

Mr Cox told the investigators that a number of ghosts had been seen in No. 44, which is 400 years old. His wife had seen a ghostly woman in black descending a staircase. In the main part of the shop, a customer had glimpsed what she described as 'a man like a headteacher' who appeared to be carrying a small boy on his shoulder. The impression lasted only a second or two. On another occasion a man had been seen walking into the back of the premises, but when pursued was found to have vanished, although the door to a

The wonderfully archaic Shambles after dark.
The medieval street boasts several haunted properties.
Shutterstock/Nando Machado

storeroom, from which there was no other exit, was standing wide open. In addition, Mr Cox said that he, as well as others, had heard a mysterious 'growling noise' in the building when no one else was around.

In No. 22 poltergeist activity was frequently met with. The invisible spook had the habit of sending items flying from the shelves and of sending display stands spinning round. A faint ringing as of hand-bells had also been detected but could never be traced to a source.

The G.H.O.S.T. team had a lively – if chilly (it was early December) – vigil in the two buildings. In No. 44 Darren felt 'several short, sharp tugs' on his trouser leg. In the cellar of No. 22 another member of the team, Fiona, felt an invisible hand touch her hip and a colleague, Simon, heard what he described as 'a low guttural breath'. A sound recorder left in an underground tunnel which stretches below the street to a church picked up a number of quite distinct but anomalous footsteps and three possible voices, each speaking a single word.

THE GHOSTS OF WHITBY

Whitby on the east coast has become a mecca for the Goth movement and fans of the macabre, largely because it was here, according to Bram Stoker's famous novel, that Count Dracula first came ashore on English soil from his home in Transylvania. For a time the vampire count stalked the streets of Whitby and its ruined abbey. In addition, of course, Whitby is simply a beautiful and wonderfully atmospheric old town.

It would be dispiriting indeed (pardon the pun) if Whitby was unable to boast a number of ghosts. But it does not disappoint. The town's best-known haunted place is also its most significant landmark, the majestic ruin of Whitby Abbey which dominates the skyline. The remains visible today date from the 13th century but there has been a church here since as long ago as Saxon times. One of the ghosts haunting the abbey is believed to date from this early period, indeed it is said to be of St Hilda, an abbess of the 7th century. In *Dracula*, published in 1897, the character Mina Harker refers to the abbey and its ghost: 'It is a most noble ruin, of immense size, and full of beautiful and romantic bits; there is a legend that a white lady is seen in one of the windows.'

According to Andy Owens, in his *Haunted Places of Yorkshire*, St Hilda's apparition is more spectacular, 'bathed in a golden glow like an angel.' Mr Owens also describes another, less attractive phantom lady haunting the abbey. This he describes as 'a dark figure, with the noticeable outline of a woman, shaking her head and wringing her hands as if

*The seaside town of Whitby, dominated by its ruined abbey, has
a number of haunted locations.*
Shutterstock/Lighttraveler

greatly upset'. She is dressed in a costume that might date from either the 18th or 19th centuries. Her identity is a mystery.

Faint singing, described by researcher John Harries as being 'in some Northumbrian dialect', has also been heard emanating from the abbey in the hour before dawn on 6 January ('Old Christmas Day'), perhaps the echo of a morning mass from long ago.

More ghostly activity has been reported from the abbey precincts. In his *Gothic Whitby*, author Colin Waters refers to a long, low building to the right of the abbey church, possibly an old barn. In the days when it was used as a Youth Hostel, the 'dark, hooded figures' of monks were sometimes seen by residents wandering from room to room and passing through solid walls. This may be the same building where a young herdsman had a vision. A shining figure appeared before the youth where he lay in a barn and told him to 'sing of the beginning of created things'. He ran to tell St Hilda of his experience and she asked him to recite the opening of Genesis. He did so, and in so doing invented plainsong. The young man became a monk and, under the name of Caedmon, became known as 'the father of English song' and the first known English poet.

Caedmon House, named after the poet, is also said to be haunted by monks, who are sometimes heard singing or chanting. Delicious savoury smells of cooking have also been detected, wafting from some unidentifiable source.

'Barguest' is a word peculiar to Yorkshire dialect and often refers to a particular type of apparition which appears in folklore throughout the British Isles: the Black Dog. As the name suggests, these spectres manifest in the form of black hounds, usually of enormous size and sometimes sporting terrifyingly fiery red eyes. Whitby had its own Black Dog, which would patrol the narrow streets and nearby moors. Anyone unlucky enough to hear its howl would be doomed to die during the following year.

According to author Ian Thompson, in his book *Dracula's Whitby*, the town was also occasionally haunted by a phantom coach. This spook would only appear after a sailor had been buried at St Mary's Church. Three days after the burial, the black coach would rattle through the town, carrying within it a company of skeletal sailors coming to pay their respects to their dead comrade. The coach would trundle three times round the grave, after which the soul of the seaman would emerge, get in and be carried away with his deceased friends.

Colin Waters describes Bagdale Hall as Whitby's oldest inhabited dwelling and also its most haunted building. Now a hotel and restaurant, the hall is a solid-looking stone-built Tudor manor house. It has enjoyed a spooky reputation for centuries. During a period of neglect in the early 1800s, passers-by would observe ghostly lights flickering behind its dusty windows. In the early 20th century, the restored house was the home of the Jeffrey family, and they reported a range of ghostly goings-on, including mysterious noises and the opening and closing of doors by invisible hands. A servant went into screaming hysterics after a feather duster was yanked from her hands by something unseen and danced about the room before her astonished eyes. The Jeffrey family left Bagdale Hall to the Whitby Literary and Philosophical Society. A sceptical town councillor attempted to spend the night alone in the building, keen to dispel its haunted reputation, but quit the place in the middle of the night, saying that the house had 'unexplainably come alive'.

The only specific ghost of Bagdale Hall is that of a Cavalier. This is thought to be of Browne Bushell, who was beheaded for treason in 1651 and whose headless apparition has been glimpsed on the upper floors. Whether his ghost is responsible for all the other paranormal activity it is hard to say.

Further ghosts of Whitby include a weeping boy in Pannett Park; a screaming woman in the former workhouse in Ropery; a spectral horse that used to gallop over the Old Bridge (now demolished); and, in Cockpit Yard, the plaintive sounds of a violin, believed to be played by the spirit of Blind Jack Metcalfe, a jovial character of the 18th century. The Old Smugglers Café and the White Horse & Griffin Hotel are also said to be haunted, but by less defined 'presences'.

A few miles from Whitby is **Robin Hood's Bay**. This former smugglers' village is an old-world concoction of winding, cobbled lanes and charming inns and cottages. It is also celebrated for its fossil-rich cliffs. The railway line above the village is said to be haunted by a headless ghost. The story goes that an old farmer and notorious miser was returning home drunk one night when he tripped over the rails and his false teeth fell out. He lay down in order to better search for them in the dark. Unfortunately, he did not notice the approaching train and he was decapitated. His head was never found and he was buried without it. His ghost supposedly now staggers about searching for his lost bonce.

An anonymous 16-year-old writing on the website About.com tells of a spooky stay in a cottage that had recently been refurbished and rented out to holidaymakers. During the holiday in 2009, he was initially given an attic bedroom to sleep in. On the first night he watched fascinated as the ceiling lamp began to spin round and round, but he then grew frightened when he realised the window was shut and there was no breeze to account for it. When his clothes, which were hanging on a rail attached to the wall, began to slip off their hangers, one by one, in consecutive order, he

St Mary's parish church, Whitby. It is said that when a seaman is buried in the churchyard, it will be visited by a company of defunct sailors in a spectral carriage.
Shutterstock/Neil Annenberg

*Robin Hood's Bay is one of the east coast's most picturesque
villages and also has its ghosts.*
Shutterstock/Gail Johnson

bolted from the room and woke up his parents. They told him to go downstairs and sleep on the sofa but after lying there for a bit he was alarmed to see a weird black fog massing behind the glass panel in the door leading to the kitchen. He ran to his parents again.

His dad grumpily stomped off to sleep in the attic room and the youngster crawled into bed with his mum. The next morning his mother admitted that she too had seen the strange fog in the kitchen and had also heard a banging about as if someone was opening and closing the cupboards. The boy continued to sleep in his mum's room and they were both unnerved by the fact that they would find the curtains had been opened or shut while they were sleeping, although they never caught them moving. Inexplicable knocking sounds and unpleasant smells also accompanied their stay in the cottage.

MORE URBAN GHOSTS

Leeds is the third largest city in England and the largest in Yorkshire. It is the cultural, financial and commercial centre of West Yorkshire, the City of Leeds forming its own metropolitan district. The city had become a major trading centre for cloth by the 18th century. The Industrial Revolution encouraged this trade to develop into manufacturing and soon vast woollen and flax mills had sprung up around the city. One of these, Armley Mills, was once the world's largest woollen mill and is now Leeds Industrial Museum. It is also one of Leeds's many haunted sites.

An invisible force has the unpleasant habit of trying to push people down a staircase in Armley Mills. A number of visitors and staff have experienced this unnerving phenomenon. Elsewhere in the museum, a female teacher taking round a party of pupils had to abandon her charges when she was overwhelmed by a feeling of pressure, a great weight on her shoulders. It felt like someone had suddenly started hanging on to her, as if to drag her down. She was so shocked and distressed by the sensation that she had to leave the building and get some fresh air. When the phenomenon struck, the teacher was passing by an old carding machine. In 1822 a boy of thirteen suffered a horrific accident when he got caught in this machine. It tore a leg from his body and he died shortly afterwards. Could this tragedy have any connection with the teacher's experience?

In Leeds city centre, two places of entertainment, the Grand Theatre and the City Varieties Music Hall, are also haunted. The Grand is as impressive as its name suggests, an imposing Victorian edifice built in 1878. Over the years, staff have reported seeing a number of apparitions in the theatre, but each only once. They include a ghostly woman in the upper circle, a caped figure in a box, a shadowy man walking down a flight of stairs and another caught on a security camera.

The City Varieties is one of the few music halls still operating in the UK and also one of the oldest: it obtained its licence in 1762. A former owner, Michael Joseph, recorded two ghosts in his theatre, 'a man in a bowler hat in old-fashioned attire' and 'a woman in white who held a lit candelabra in her right hand'. Both were seen near the piano on the stage. Kenneth Goor, who has spent years researching and guiding people round 'the dark side of Leeds', is a Friend of the City

Varieties Music Hall and has had the opportunity to set down a number of spooky happenings here. In his book on *Haunted Leeds*, he describes: a lady in crinoline in the bar; 'a woman wearing old-fashioned clothing hunched over a washbasin' in the ladies' loo; another phantom lady in a box; a man wearing a bowler hat and a trench coat in the upper circle; and a pair of legs minus a body walking up to the upper circle.

One member of staff has reported hearing disembodied footsteps and the faint sound of a piano in the theatre. More bizarrely, this same man once saw a magician's cabinet shuffle towards him across the stage. Another witness reported hearing an odd 'huffing noise' and warm breath on the back of his neck when he was walking near the dressing rooms. Neither came from any visible source.

There are many other notable buildings in Leeds city centre which are claimed to be haunted. These include its imposing Town Hall, where the ghost is believed to be of the incongruously named Charlie Peace, a murderous thief of the 19th century. Peace shot a policeman and the husband of a woman he fancied, among others, before being caught and hanged. For a time he was held in the old cells below the Town Hall and it is here that his angry spirit is said to haunt.

In 1994 the press reported sightings of a 'white lady' at the building which now houses both the County and Crown courts. According to Kenneth Goor, however, what was actually seen was the apparition of an elderly man dressed in grey. He was seen walking through a door into a courtroom (without opening it) and, on several other occasions, 'crouching' in a corner outside the room. His identity remains a mystery. He was described as 'ordinary-looking' but with a dead white face; the cut of his clothes seemed fairly modern.

During the 1880s the ghost of a former librarian was seen on a number of occasions in the library in Commercial Street. It was first seen by John Macalister, who took over as librarian in 1884. He was leaving late one night when he saw at the end of a short passage a man's face peering at him out of the darkness. Thinking he had surprised a thief, Mr Macalister hurried back to his room and armed himself with a revolver. Then he returned to the main book room and called out to the intruder to show himself.

The grand Town Hall in Leeds, which is haunted by the spirit of a murderer.
Shutterstock/Shahid Ali Khan

*An illustration from The Strand Magazine showing the ghost sighting in the library
in Commercial Street, Leeds, in 1884. Image © Richard Holland*

'Then,' recalled Mr Macalister, 'I saw a face, looking round
one of the bookcases. I say "looking" round, but it had an
odd appearance, as if the body were in the bookcase. The
face was pallid and hairless and the orbits of the eyes were
deep. I advanced towards it and as I did so I saw an old man
with high shoulders. He seemed to rotate out of the end of
the bookcase and with his back towards me and with a
shuffling gait, walk rather quickly from the bookcase to the

door of a small lavatory which opened from the library and
had no other access. I followed the man at once into the
lavatory and to my extreme surprise found no one there.'

Mr Macalister later discovered that the face he had seen
belonged to his immediate predecessor, who had died at the
early age of 48. This story first appeared in an article by
Beckles Willson, a member of the fledgling Society for
Psychical Research, in the December 1908 edition of *The
Strand Magazine* (a copy of which is in the author's collection).
The locality of the library and all the names were suppressed
by Mr Willson, but Kenneth Goor's research firmly places
the scene at the Commercial Street Library and restores the
names of two assistants who experienced further strange
phenomena in the library in 1889. The only discrepancy is in
the name of the ghost: the recently deceased librarian is
referred to as 'Mr Q—-' in Willson's article but in fact it
appears to have been a Mr Sternberg. More details of this
fascinating case can be found in Mr Goor's *Haunted Leeds*.

Another ghost popped up unexpectedly in the Leeds suburb
of Moortown in 1970 during the building of a synagogue.
According to veteran ghost-hunter the late Andrew Green,
the spook calmly watched the builders in broad daylight
while they were excavating a trench. In his book *Our Haunted
Kingdom*, Green quotes the foreman, a Mr Edgar Lupton: 'It
was just the top half of one of those old Quakers, dressed in
a charcoal grey cloak and wearing a wide-brimmed hat with
a flat top.'

The apparition faded away before his eyes but was seen again
the following day by another builder in another part of the

construction site. The synagogue was being built near the ruins of Donisthorpe Hall which, at the end of its life, had been a home for elderly Jews. The ghost is more likely to have been that of a rabbi – the cloak and wide-brimmed hat are consistent – rather than a Quaker. No doubt it was simply showing an interest in the construction of a temple dedicated to its faith.

Sheffield is the administrative centre of South Yorkshire. A major manufacturing town, Sheffield was world-famous for its metal-working: steel, cutlery and the unique 'Sheffield Plate' silverware. In common with Leeds, the city has a haunted library. In the art deco Central Library building, a librarian had a shock a few years ago when she saw, not a disembodied head as at Leeds, but a disembodied arm! She was working alone in a storeroom in the basement when she felt something clutch at her skirt. She spun round to see an arm emerging from a bookcase, the hand twitching and shuddering in a peculiar and horrible manner. The librarian scarcely had time to react to the bizarre and ghastly nature of what she was seeing when the arm 'fell limp and then faded out'. The arm has never appeared again but in the same room other members of staff have heard a guttural sound like the death rattle of a dying man. The library was built on the site of a Medical School, which may partly explain the presence of these eerie manifestations.

Sheffield can also boast a haunted theatre. A former manager is thought to be one of the ghosts of the Lyceum. He is described by the authors of *Haunted Sheffield* ('Mr and Mrs P. Dreadful') as 'dressed in a straw boater hat, flannel trousers, striped jacket, handlebar moustache and carrying a cane'. He first made his presence known during a major refurbishment programme in the 1980s. He seemed curious to know what was going on at the theatre and watched electricians as they worked. Since then he has been seen on a number of other occasions by stage hands. He has also been blamed for rearranging props on the stage while no one is looking.

The remaining two ghosts of the Lyceum Theatre are the Grey Lady and 'Ben', a character believed to date from the Music Hall which formerly stood here. Ben is a hulking but amiable figure who almost uniquely can be smelled as well as seen: he has an unwashed and earthy aroma about him. The Grey Lady is a sadder figure. Her story is that she fell madly in love with a leading man only to be publicly jilted by him. She was unable to bear the humiliation and hanged herself in the theatre. The Grey Lady has been seen in various parts of the Lyceum, most often in a dressing room or sitting in her favourite seat in the balcony. She has also been heard weeping.

The splendid Town Hall in Sheffield City Centre is possessed of one of those anonymous, never-seen entities that enjoys making a nuisance of itself. It haunts a back kitchen and has upset staff by spreading tea, sugar and other foodstuffs around when the room has been left empty, in one case for only a few minutes. It has the annoying habit of switching on kettles and leaving them to boil dry. This was seen to happen even when it was switched off: the kettle continued boiling away.

Sheffield's magnificent Victorian Town Hall is possessed of a poltergeist in a back kitchen.
Shutterstock/Alastair Wallace

Another council property, Leader House, also has a troublesome ghost. Leader House was built in 1780 for a wealthy silver-plater, Thomas Leader, and the ghost is believed to be a maid dating from its time as a private home. The ghost seems to resent the presence of other women in the house. She has a habit of pestering cleaners, turning off their vacuum cleaners and blowing cold air in their faces. In 2001 she targeted an archivist, reducing her to tears after locking her in a room and causing filing cabinets to shake in an alarming manner. The maid's phantom has been seen staring out of a bay window overlooking the Central Library. She has also been seen outside Leader House, making her way down Surrey Street from the pavement in front of the Graduate pub. The Graduate also boasts a woman in black who patrols an upper floor.

Sheffield has a number of other haunted pubs. These include the Brown Bear in Norfolk Street, haunted by a coachman who killed himself after breaking both his legs in an accident; the Three Tuns, Silver Street Head, haunted by a nun; the timber-framed Old Queen's Head in Pond Street which has a 'presence' in the ladies loo; and The Market Tavern, Exchange Street, which is haunted by a brave collier who left his drink to return to help a child trapped in the mine but who lost his own life in the attempt. Sadly, the latter pub closed a year or two ago but there is hope that it will be preserved rather than just swept away by development.

Sheffield also has its own Barguest. This one used to patrol the six-hundred-year-old Campo Lane. An odd incident, recorded in *Haunted Sheffield*, suggests that it may have been encountered as recently as 1999. According to the authors, one of two students returning home past the Botanical Gardens was set upon by a big black dog, which knocked him over and appeared to maul him. It then ran off and vanished into thin air crossing Campo Lane. The young man appeared to be unhurt but during the subsequent hours scratches and bite-marks appeared on his skin.

Finally, we must mention Sheffield Cathedral. This handsome parish church became a cathedral in 1914. Here a young woman in Elizabethan costume has been seen strolling past the rood screen on Sundays. It is assumed to be some other, mischievous spirit which has the habit of playing with the lights in the building. Numerous times the cathedral has been seen to be blazing with light just minutes after it has been locked up in darkness. The same spook may also be responsible for blowing out devotional candles and for the ruffling of the regimental flags in the Chapel of St George. This latter phenomenon has been seen to occur no matter how still the air is.

The modest cathedral city of **Ripon** (North Yorkshire) has a haunted house right in its centre. This is the ancient Wakeman's House. The Wakeman was employed to blow a horn at the start of the night watch, when watchmen would then start patrolling the city. The last Wakeman was Hugh Ripley. He lost his job in 1604 but was made mayor instead. The tradition was revived in the 1920s and a gentleman in 18th-century costume continues to give three ceremonial blasts on a horn at night. Wakeman's House was Hugh Ripley's home and is now a museum and café. In 1923, when the custom was revived, a crowd gathered to hear the new Wakeman blow his horn. Suddenly, one of the bystanders

An Elizabethan woman is one of the ghosts of Sheffield Cathedral.
Shutterstock/Tom Curtis

A headless ghost used to ride in the air above the streets of Beverley, punishment for riding his horse into Beverley Minster.
Shutterstock/Daniel J. Rao

cried out that he could see a white face peering down from the top room of Wakeman's House. Many others saw it too, and a few thought it was smiling. Was it the ghost of Hugh Wakeman?

Before Wakeman's House was reopened, it was known to be haunted. Disembodied footsteps were regularly reported by people staying here at night and one night an indistinct figure was seen crossing a bedroom. The following evening the witness arranged a row of chairs so that they blocked the way the apparition had taken: in the morning he found they had all been pushed aside.

Beverley is the historic administrative centre of the East Riding of Yorkshire, famous for its magnificent Minster. Centuries ago a reckless nobleman by the name of Sir

Josceline Percy had the temerity to ride his horse through the door of the Minster, where it then galloped about the aisles. After death he was punished for this sacrilege. His headless ghost was doomed to ride around in a phantom coach above the streets of Beverley until the hundred nails in a massive chest dropped out, which they did, once a year. In Norfolk Street a former gaol, now converted to private homes, was haunted by a prisoner who had committed suicide. His appearances were so ghastly that he was considered a useful deterrent to criminals.

The larger city of **Kingston upon Hull** also has its ghosts. As recently as 2012 they were making the news. The presence known as 'Beryl' by the landlady and regulars of the Manchester Arms in Scale Lane seemingly made an appearance on the pub's CCTV cameras. 'I could definitely make out a lady on the screen,' the landlady told the *Hull Daily Mail*. Previously 'Beryl' had remained invisible, but had made her presence known by interfering with the electrics and the plumbing. She also had the unnerving habit of running her icy fingers through people's hair.

Another invisible spook haunts the George Hotel in Hull's Old Town. In 2013 the George had just undergone an extensive scheme of redecoration and the new owners reported hearing something running up and down a flight of stairs. They were also puzzled by a 'strong smell of fire' in the building. Staff of a hair salon in Whitefriargate became so distressed by the persistent sounds of footsteps pacing about an upper room that they called the police. The room was rigged out with trip-wires. The next time the footsteps were heard, the police threw open the door, only to find the room empty, the trip-wires intact and the light now on.

In the centre of **Bradford**, West Yorkshire, is Paper Hall. Paper Hall was built in 1648 as a private home and is the oldest domestic building in the city. It is thought that the Industrial Revolution started in Bradford at Paper Hall with the introduction of hand-used spinning machines in its attic. The origin of its peculiar name is a mystery, however. The house is haunted by a former owner, an admiral who was murdered nearby. He had a wooden leg, so the spooky footsteps heard clumping up and down the stairs have a distinctive sound.

In 1926 there was panic in the Bradford suburbs when a frightening hooded 'apparition' put the Manchester Road and Bierley districts under siege. According to Jack Hallam, who relates the tale in his *Ghosts of the North*, women were warned not go out after dark and the police were called out in force to hunt it down.

Writes Hallam: 'Once the apparition was glimpsed on the roof of a local brewery at the side of a chimney-stack, but it vanished when policemen turned their torches on it. Several nights later it was seen moving among the tombstones in Bierley cemetery. After one woman had suffered a severe shock through seeing the figure peering at her through a window, elderly residents of Bradford remembered that a similar haunting was reported in the locality.'

Sightings and other spooky incidents occurred for more than a year and then, as all such scares tend to do, it fizzled out, the enigma unexplained. The hooded spectre has not been seen since.

Bradford's oddly named Paper Hall was built in the 17th century and is now used as business premises. It is haunted by the ghost of a murdered seaman.
Shutterstock/Alastair Wallace

Staying in West Yorkshire, **Huddersfield** has a number of 'ghosted' locations, many first set down by one Philip Ahier in the 1940s and added to more recently by Mr Kai Roberts in his *Haunted Huddersfield*. The town's grand railway station is said to be haunted by a bad-tempered porter on whom any inexplicable and annoying incident tends to be blamed. A murdered girl haunts the long stretch of canal in the Standedge Tunnel. The ghost of 'Black Dick', otherwise a notorious nobleman of the 17th century named Sir Richard Beaumont, made a nuisance of itself throughout the region which has since become the suburb of Kirkheaton but its troublesome ways came to an end some time ago.

Halifax Town Hall is another of Yorkshire's impressive Victorian administrative centres able to boast a ghost.
Shutterstock/jennyt

Among the many ghosts of **Halifax** is the entity seen peering out of the spire of Square Chapel. No one knows who or what it is but it has been photographed on more than one occasion. The Town Hall – as grand as any other in Yorkshire – is haunted by a former mayor, resplendent in his scarlet robes of office. The 17th-century Old Cock Inn is haunted by a chambermaid and her baby. In Crown Street, former newspaper offices are haunted by a man who was murdered by a maniac using a hatchet and, of all things, a dumbbell. Murder also explains the ghosts of the Piece Hall, a splendid commercial centre built in Palladian style in the 18th century. They are the spirits of merchants slain for their money.

Finally, according to local man Malcolm Hanson, Sheep Street, **Skipton** (North Yorkshire) can boast 'the most haunted street in Yorkshire'. Mr Hanson, who organises Ghost Walks in the town, set himself the task of 'interviewing every person who lived or worked along this singular 300-yard stretch'. He learned that a ghostly woman dressed in pink haunts the cellar of the Woolly Sheep pub; the apparition of a small girl clutching a teddy bear has frequently been seen by staff at a nearby shop; a disembodied voice has been heard in another shop; 'Mr Crump the Chemist', who hanged himself in the attic of a neighbouring building, still makes his presence known; and the ghost of a sobbing old lady haunts the end of Sheep Street at Manby's Corner. Mr Hanson also spoke to a young couple who described a terrifying encounter in the street with 'a man dressed all in black with red eyes', who 'floated right up to them before suddenly shooting up the ginnel to Victoria Square'.

THE HOUSE OF THE SKULL

Burton Agnes Hall is one of Yorkshire's most magnificent stately homes. A grand Elizabethan mansion, it is situated in the East Riding between Bridlington and Driffield. The Hall has remained in the same family for fifteen generations and boasts fine furniture and *objets d'art* dating from throughout its history, including works of art acquired by successive owners of the house. The latter include an important collection of paintings by the French Impressionists. Burton Agnes Hall is still a private home but is open to the public. Other attractions include award-winning gardens, a woodland walk, the remains of the original Norman manor house and even a medieval church (visit www.burtonagnes.com for more information).

But as John Ingram, in his pioneering work on *Haunted Homes and Family Legends*, puts it: 'There is, however a skeleton, or, rather, a portion of one, in this splendid mansion.'

The 'portion' of the skeleton he refers to is the skull of 'Owd Nance', whose ghost has walked the house for centuries. In life, 'Owd Nance' was Anne Griffiths, the youngest of three sisters who commissioned the building of Burton Agnes Hall during the reign of Elizabeth I. At the time they had been living in an earlier Norman house, which Anne in particular

Burton Agnes Hall in the East Riding is one of Yorkshire's grandest houses, but is as well known for its ghost as for its Elizabethan architecture.

felt was too small and not nearly showy enough for a family as important as she considered hers to be. Anne followed the construction of the new mansion with excitement, often stating that she could hardly wait to move into it. Before she had the chance, however, tragedy struck.

Anne was waylaid by robbers one night. Although her cries for help brought villagers running to her aid, she had suffered a mortal blow to the head before she was rescued. Anne was carried back home, where she lay dying and fretting that she was no longer able to visit the work in progress at the new house. Her one fear was that she would pass away before having the chance to see its glorious completion. When it became apparent she had only a few days left to live, Anne made a very strange request of her sisters.

'Sisters,' she said, 'never shall I sleep peacefully in my grave unless I, or a part of me at least, remain in our beautiful home as long as it lasts. Promise me this, dear sisters, that when I am dead my head shall be taken from my body and preserved within the walls. Here let it for ever remain, and on no account be removed. And understand and make it known to those who in future will become possessors of the house, that if they disobey this my last injunction, my spirit shall, if so able and so permitted, make such a disturbance within its walls as to render it uninhabitable for others so long as my head is divorced from its home.'

At the time this bizarre injunction was taken as the ramblings of delirium and although Anne's sisters, in order to calm her, promised to carry out it out, they had no true intention of doing so. When she died, Anne's unmutilated body was laid to rest in its entirety beneath a slab within the church.

One evening, soon after Anne's sisters had moved into the splendid new house at Burton Agnes, they were startled by a loud bang from an upstairs room. They rushed upstairs in great consternation, imagining that a heavy article of furniture had fallen over. Nothing, however, could be found out of place. Puzzled and somewhat unnerved, the Griffiths sisters retired to bed, unaware that they had just experienced the overture to what would become a paranormal persecution of unearthly noises. On the same night of the

A sketch made by Charles Harper in 1907 of a painting of the three Griffiths sisters which hangs in Burton Agnes Hall. Anne is on the right.

week following, the household was disturbed by sounds as if dozens of doors were being opened and slammed and as if crowds of invisible people were running up and down the corridors. This was repeated on a weekly basis, with the disturbances inevitably ceasing with a 'groaning as from a dying person'.

The servants fled the house and the sisters were at their wits' end. Then it was pointed out to them that paranormal activity took place on the same night of the week that Anne had died. Was she now making her displeasure known at their broken promise from beyond the grave? So distressed were the family that they took the extreme action of exhuming Anne's body. The story goes that on opening her coffin they were amazed and horrified to discover that although Anne's body had barely begun to decompose, her head had already become a fleshless skull and had detached itself from the neck. The indication seemed all too clear. With great reverence they carried the skull to Burton Agnes Hall and placed it in view on a little table. The ghostly disturbances ceased and the house remained untroubled for the entire time the skull was allowed to remain in the house.

Burton Agnes Hall is one of the best known of a number of 'skull houses' in Britain. There are numerous legends of 'screaming skulls', as they are known, and most follow the pattern of the Burton Agnes story: someone insists on their death-bed that their skull be left in the house they loved or where they were murdered, with unearthly disturbances following whenever it is moved or removed. It appears to have been an ancient tradition to keep a skull in a house as a good-luck charm or protection against malign forces, a tradition which might date back to Roman times or even before. The 'screaming skull' of Bettiscombe Manor in Dorset has a similar historical legend as that of Burton Agnes to explain its presence, but tests have shown that the artefact is actually thousands of years old and probably came originally from a prehistoric burial mound.

Anne Griffiths' skull is also said to have 'screamed' and caused other nuisances over the years, especially after the Boynton family succeeded by marriage to possession of Burton Agnes. A journalist, F. Ross, writing in the 19th century, stated: 'Many attempts have since been made to rid the Hall of the skull, but without success; as whenever it has been removed the ghostly knockings have been resumed, and no rest or peace enjoyed until it has been restored.

'On one occasion a maid-servant threw it from the window upon a passing load of manure, but from that moment the horses were not able to move the waggon an inch, and despite the vigorous whipping of the waggoner, all their efforts were in vain, until the servant confessed what she had done, when the skull was brought back into the house, and the horses drew the waggon along without the least difficulty.

An illustration from the early 1900s showing the attempts to dispose of the Burton Agnes Hall skull.

On another, one of the Boyntons caused it to be buried in the garden, when the most dismal wailings and cries kept the house in a state of disquietude and alarm until it was dug up and restored to its place in the Hall, where they ceased.'

Even when the skull was left unmolested, 'Owd Nance' had a habit of walking round Burton Agnes Hall at night. Her particular haunt was the Queen's State Bedroom, where she would appear wearing a blue gown. Many years ago Anne's skull was hidden away in a secret compartment in the house to prevent it from being interfered with again. Its whereabouts are now a mystery.

MORE HAUNTED HOUSES

Haworth Parsonage is one of the most visited houses in Yorkshire, for it was, of course, the home of the Brontë sisters. Together with their brother Branwell, Charlotte, Emily and Anne formed an extraordinary cultural powerhouse in this formerly obscure West Yorkshire village. Emily and Charlotte wrote two of the greatest novels in English literature, *Wuthering Heights* and *Jane Eyre*, as well as other significant works, and Anne contributed notable novels of her own, such as *The Tenant of Wildfell Hall*.

The house is now the Brontë Parsonage Museum and is open to the public. Many visitors have reported feeling 'presences' around the house, as if they are being watched, and one recently took a photograph of the frontage only to notice in it a dark, human-sized shape in the doorway where no one had been standing when she pressed the shutter. Tradition states that Emily Brontë returns on the anniversary of her death, 19 December. Charlotte too is said to haunt the house; she wasted away here from a protracted illness in 1855. The sisters' ghosts have also been seen on the walk behind the Parsonage which leads up to a little waterfall on the moors, a favourite resort of theirs.

Bolling Hall might reasonably have been included in the 'More Urban Ghosts' chapter, for it is situated just a mile from the city centre of Bradford. It is a haven of peace, however, situated in a quiet, leafy garden. Parts of the building date back to medieval times and it is now a museum. In 1643, during the height of the Civil War, Parliamentarian Bradford was laid siege by Royalist forces. Their commander, William Cavendish, Duke of Newcastle, made Bolling Hall his headquarters. The Duke was determined to end the siege and ordered his soldiers to break through and slaughter every man, woman and child within swords' reach. The night before the proposed massacre, however, Cavendish had an encounter with the supernatural. The clothes were torn from his bed three times and a ghostly woman in white appeared at the foot of his bed. The apparition wrung its hands and cried 'Pity poor Bradford!' Cavendish was so awe-struck that he immediately countermanded his cruel order.

On 22 August 1861, another ghost appeared at Bolling Hall, just once. Richard Oastler, remembered as a campaigner for factory reform, often visited the house and on one occasion got into an argument with a member of the family over the existence of an afterlife. Oastler promised that he'd come back as a ghost to prove his point – and apparently he did so, appearing in front of Bolling Hall on the day of his death.

The spirit of Wuthering Heights author Emily Brontë is said return to Haworth on the anniversary of her death.

Sunderlandwick Hall, near Driffield, is a working farm on a site that dates back to the Bronze Age. An abandoned medieval village on the estate has recently been made a scheduled monument by English Heritage. The ghost is an unusual one: the sound of wet feet slapping along a stone-flagged corridor. The reason for this odd manifestation has unfortunately been lost over the years.

Another peculiar phenomenon is said to occur at **Hawksworth Hall**, near Guiseley. Here the hand-print of a child has been found mysteriously impressed on pillows in one of the bedrooms. The identity of this intriguing spook is unknown, nor why he or she should leave such a mark. The other two ghosts of Hawksworth Hall are more traditional and equally anonymous: a Grey Lady and a monk who wander the corridors at night. The Hall is now a school and is closed to the public.

The mark left behind by a ghost at **Oakwell Hall**, in the village of Birstall, West Yorkshire, was a gorier relic than the gentle example at Hawksworth. In December 1684, the front door was thrown open and William Batt, eldest son of the family then in residence, strode in, his face pale, his eyes wild. His family stared in astonishment as William, without a word to anyone, passed them by and staggered up the main staircase. Amazed by their son's unexpected appearance, the Batts hurried after him, but then drew back in dismay when they saw a splash of fresh blood on the stairs. Family and servants rushed up the stairs but found that William was nowhere to be seen. After a search, they returned downstairs, full of foreboding. The bloodstain too was found to have vanished. The Batts later learned the shocking news that

'Pity poor Bradford!' Bolling Hall, from a 19th-century illustration.

William had been murdered in London on the day they saw his apparition.

Oakwell Hall is now a 'living museum', the interior recreated to look as it might have done in the Batts' time. This authenticity may be the reason the spirit of William Batt is still perceived around the house. After his murder, he haunted the Hall for some time but has been quieter since an exorcism was carried out.

At Timble, near Harrogate, is **Swinsty Hall**, one of the few Grade I-listed homes in private hands. It is a handsome mansion, more than four centuries old. Some years ago, the then resident family, the Cuckstons, reported a wide range of paranormal activity at Swinsty Hall. The ghost – which

The stately home of Ripley Castle has been in the hands of the same family for more than seven centuries. One of them has remained behind as a ghost.
Shutterstock/Phil MacD Photography

they never saw – seemed to think it was part of the family. It would call out the names of Mr and Mrs Cuckston from somewhere at the top of the stairs. One night, when Mrs Cuckston woke up feeling cold, a comforting blanket was settled over her but the following morning her puzzled husband denied putting it there. Even creepier was the occasion when Mrs Cuckston was in the bedroom waiting for her husband to finish watching his TV programme downstairs: she apparently heard him come in and felt his weight beside her as he got into bed. A few minutes later, however, she rolled over to find no one lying there – her husband was still downstairs.

Scotton Old Hall in Nidderdale. It is the latter place he now haunts, patrolling the corridors. His ghost has also been seen in the lanes near the house. Another celebrity, Mary, Queen of Scots, is said to haunt **Nappa Hall**, a mile east of Askrigg, Wensleydale. Mary stayed briefly in the Hall during her lengthy period in custody by the English. A visitor to the house in 1878 encountered a ghostly woman in black velvet in the west tower. Her face, he said, 'was very lovely' and reminded him strongly of pictures he had seen of Mary, Queen of Scots, hence the identification with her, although the ghost may in fact be of a less well-known character in the house's long history. (Please note that both Scotton and Nappa Halls are private homes.)

Not far away is **Ripley Castle**. Here the ghost is of Elizabeth Ingilby, who was known as the 'Nun of Ghent' for her piety and whose portrait hangs at the top of the stairs. She is a very polite ghost. She knocks at bedroom doors but will only enter if the occupant calls out 'Come in!' The Ingilby family enjoyed a colourful history. They were staunch Royalists and Catholics, and one of the women of the house rode into battle during the Civil War while another kept a gun trained on Oliver Cromwell when he made an unwelcome visit to the Hall. Francis Ingilby was executed for continuing to hold the Mass during the reign of Elizabeth I. After James I stayed in the house, the family set about plotting to kill him – nine of the eleven conspirators of the Gunpowder Plot were close relatives or associates of the Ingilbys. The Ingilby family is still in residence at Ripley Castle and organised tours are available.

The most famous Gunpowder Plotter of them all, Guido Fawkes, was a frequent visitor at Ripley Castle and also at

Rossington Hall, near Doncaster, has two ghosts. One is known as 'Annie' and has been identified as Annette Streatfield, who inherited the house in 1931 but died just six years later. According to author Antony Hippisley Coxe, a male figure, fancily dressed in top hat and frock coat, haunts the grounds, apparently inspecting the stables. Rossington Hall was all but destroyed by fire in the 19th century but, having been rebuilt, is now a fine example of the Victorian country house. It is run as a 'wedding, events and dining venue'.

The Grey Lady of **East Riddlesden Hall**, a National Trust property near Keighley, remains entirely anonymous but it's thought she must be responsible for the weird occurrence said to take place every New Year's Eve. On that date an old wooden cradle, kept in the house for three hundred years, rocks inexplicably, as if moved by an invisible hand. A ghostly face has also been seen peering through a rose window at the top of the stairs. This is the apparition either of a wool merchant murdered by a butler for the gold he carried, or of the murderous butler himself (opinions are divided).

Shibden Hall, near Halifax, was built in 1420 and is now open to the public, managed by Calderdale Council. At the heart of the house is a vast oak table constructed within the hall as it was being built and which has never been moved since. According to the 'Ghosts and Legends of the Lower Calder Valley' blog run by Kai Roberts, numerous ghosts have been reported at Shibden Hall. They include a Grey Lady, a coach drawn by a headless coachman, a girl who was drowned in a nearby pond and a cat which was seen to pad

Numerous ghosts have been reported from medieval Shibden Hall near Halifax.
Shutterstock/Alastair Wallace

effortlessly through a wall. A 'nebulous black shape' has also been encountered by a curator and the inexplicable aroma of pipe smoke has been detected in the cellar.

The most persistent ghost is that of Ann Walker, who inherited the hall from her lover Anne Lister. Ann had long struggled with mental health issues, quite possibly exacerbated by the fact that she was a lesbian in the mid-19th century, a time when homosexuality was not understood and, between men, ruthlessly repressed. She became a recluse at Shibden and was allegedly found covered in blood and surrounded by rotting food. She ended her days in an asylum.

Lord Halifax, whose two *Ghost Books* published in the 1930s have become important resources for enthusiasts of the paranormal, lived for some years at **Temple Newsam House**, near Leeds. It is fitting, then, that this splendid Tudor-Jacobean mansion also has its ghosts. Lord Halifax saw one ghost during his residency at Temple Newsam: the Blue Lady. According to Jack Hallam: 'One winter's night, when he was unable to sleep, he saw the Blue Lady, an elderly woman in a blue gown over which was draped a lace shawl. By the light of the fire he watched from his bed as she crossed the Blue Damask bedroom to the dressing room adjoining. When he lit a candle, there was nothing to be seen.'

The name 'Temple' Newsam comes from the fact that in the 12th century, long before the house was built, the estate was farmed by the Knights Templar. A Templar knight is one of Temple Newsam's many ghosts. In addition there is the apparition of a small boy, who emerges from a cupboard in the north wing, and a 'malevolent-looking' monk in the Long Gallery. A door to one room in the south wing has the habit of opening and closing by itself. Strange noises, as of furniture being moved about, have been heard in the room below. More disturbing is the sound heard emanating from the Red Room. It has been described as 'the screams of someone in agony'. Temple Newsam is managed by Leeds City Council and is open to the public.

Finally, we must consider the gruesome legend of **Calverley Old Hall**. Calverley is a village a few miles north-west of Leeds and north-east of Bradford. At the heart of it can be found its original medieval manor house, a pleasing jumble

*Temple Newsam House is the former home of ghost story collector Lord
Halifax and is suitably haunted.*
Shutterstock/: Tom Curtis

of sandstone buildings, parts of which date back to the 13th
century. It is now in the care of the Landmark Trust and one
wing is let as a holiday cottage to help raise funds for its
restoration.

Centuries ago a horrible tragedy took place at Calverley Old
Hall. In 1604 the house was owned by Master Walter
Calverley, described as 'a wild and reckless man'. He was
prone to gambling and had all but bankrupted himself. On
23 April of that year his mind snapped and he arrived at the
hall in a 'frenzy' of rage. He snatched up one of his children,
then the other, and stabbed them to death with his dagger.
He committed a similar assault on his distraught wife.
Leaving her for dead, he then went in search of his third
child, a baby out at wet-nurse in a neighbouring village. The

strong corsets worn by his wife had been sufficient to deflect the blow of Calverley's blade and she was able to raise the alarm. Her insane husband was pursued by villagers; his horse shied; he was thrown to the ground and his murderous rampage came to an end. He was placed in custody.

While in prison a semblance of sanity returned to Walter Calverley. Under the laws of the day, his property would be claimed by the Crown for his misdeeds. The only way to keep Calverley Hall in the family's possession, eventually to be claimed by the infant son he had sought to kill, was by taking advantage of a loophole in the law. He refused to plead, forcing the court to torture him into a confession via an archaic ruling called *pein forte et dure* ('strong and harsh punishment'). We have already encountered this form of punishment in the story of St Margaret Clitherow in York. Master Walter was stretched out and a board laid over his body. The board was then loaded with heavy boulders. Suffocating, his ribs cracking and in great agony, Walter still refused to admit his guilt. Struggling for breath, he begged a loyal servant to sit on the board, so as to increase the weight upon him to a fatal degree. The weeping servant complied and Calverley was suffocated.

Walter Calverley had therefore died without having been found guilty of the crime of murder. His estates were handed over to his widow. The magistrates were furious at being cheated out of their prize, as they saw it. They ordered the unfortunate servant who had helped end his master's agony to be hanged in his place!

Calverley Hall, as illustrated in Charles Harper's book on Haunted Houses published in 1907.

After such a catalogue of horror and drama, it is no wonder Calverley Hall and its surroundings gained the reputation of being haunted. Walter Calverley returned as a ghost, galloping about the countryside after dark on a headless horse. Accompanying him were a number of other spectral horsemen. Together they became a terror to the neighbourhood and would 'run down any poor benighted folks who happened to be thereabouts'. The local vicar had a go at exorcising the troublesome spooks but with limited success.

One night the bell of the village church was rung repeatedly by an invisible agency. It went on tolling for a long time as the villagers stood around shivering from more than just the coldness of the night. They were unable to gain access to the church because the door refused to open. It only unjammed itself when the ringing ceased as mysteriously as it had begun. The phenomenon was presumed to be the work of

Walter Calverley's ghost. Calverley was also blamed for the uncomfortable experience had by a Wesleyan preacher who spent a night in the house.

'I had had not been asleep long before I thought something crept up to my breast, pressing me much,' wrote the Revd Richard Burdsall. 'I was greatly agitated and struggled hard to awake. In this situation, according to the best judgment I could form, the bed seemed to swing as if it had been slung in slings, and I was thrown out on the floor.'

The Revd Burdsall made two further attempts to get back to sleep but on each occasion he was thrown out of the bed, between the mattress and the covers like the slippery contents of a sandwich. For years, too, other paranormal echoes of the tragedy were believed to exist in Calverley Hall: irremovable blood stains on the floor of the room where the murders took place and, considerably more abstruse, a single flagstone in the cellar which was wet to the touch while all those around it remained dry. What this uninspiring phenomenon has to do with either the murders or the ghost is hard to say, but Yorkshire journalist William Scruton assured his readers in 1884: 'Wise men have tried to account for this; but, as yet, have signally failed. Here it is plain to be seen, and what one sees, one can believe.'

Believe what? He does not say.

GHOSTS AMONG THE RUINS

There are a vast number of historic sites in Yorkshire but many alas are not in the state of preservation enjoyed by the manor houses just discussed. **Heath Old Hall**, near Wakefield, for example, is in a ruinous state. Originally constructed in the 1500s, it later became the home of the indomitable Lady Mary Bolles, who died in the 1660s. Lady Mary's spirit continued to intimidate the household long after her death, making a particular nuisance of herself whenever alterations were made to the house that she didn't approve of. Her ghost was seen not only in the house but also in a grove of chestnut trees that led down to the river and elsewhere in the grounds. Now known as 'the Blue Lady', the ghost is still said to haunt the ruins.

On the way up to Ingleborough (the highest peak in the Yorkshire Dales) from Clapham can be found the remains of **Clapdale Hall**. The ruin is haunted by Dame Alice Kytell (or Kyteler), who escaped from Ireland after being condemned as a witch.

Very little of **Skipsea Castle** survives beyond the Norman bailey (or mound) on which it was erected. Skipsea is located by the East Yorkshire coast, rather closer than it was when it was built, for the sea here has encroached considerably over the centuries. The castle was given by William the Conqueror to one of his right-hand men, Drogo de Bevere, a cruel man, known for indiscriminate acts of violence and a taste for torture. Fortunately it is not he who haunts Skipsea Castle but the quiet spirit of his long-suffering wife, whom he also killed. The murder was covered up and Lady de Bevere's body buried beneath the castle's cellar. Ever since, Lady de Bevere's sad ghost has wandered round the castle site in the hope that someone will find her bones, give them a proper burial and say a Mass for her soul.

Further north is the more impressive ruin of **Scarborough Castle**, dramatically situated on a rocky promontory overlooking the sea. The castle is haunted by Piers Gaveston, the favourite and probable lover of King Edward II. Gaveston's influence over the king made him many enemies and in 1312 he was eventually cornered at Scarborough by rebellious barons and beheaded. Gaveston's headless phantom creeps about the battlements and has the dangerous habit of rushing at people in the hope of frightening them into headlong flight, over the edge.

If visiting Scarborough Castle, beware of one of Britain's more dangerous ghosts, that of Piers Gaveston, First Earl of Cornwall.
Shutterstock/ronfromyork

Gaveston may have lost his head but the spook of **Spofforth Castle** is just as literally legless. Only the upper half of the ghost is seen. Andy Owens, in his *Haunted Places of Yorkshire*, describes it as 'the bluish-white apparition of the top half of a woman'. It appears near the top of a tower among the ruins of this largely 15th-century castle south-east of Harrogate and then falls to the ground. Who she was in life and whether she jumped or was pushed from the tower remain unknown.

Pickering Castle on the North York Moors also has an anonymous ghost, that of a monk. Why a monk should be haunting a Norman fortress is a bit of a mystery but he may have been in the private employ of a former owner, to hear confession and to hold masses. He is seen briskly walking across the open space towards the keep.

A ghostly monk has also been glimpsed at **Conisbrough Castle** in South Yorkshire. He may possibly have some connection with the mysterious lights which hover about near the old chapel. The castle was built by the Normans and boasts an especially impressive keep. A White Lady haunts the very top of the keep, from which, legend has it, she was pushed to her death. Disembodied footsteps have also been heard in the keep. Conisbrough Castle is now in the care of English Heritage.

The ruins of **Richmond Castle**, in North Yorkshire, are particularly fine and English Heritage holds numerous heritage-themed events within its walls. Weird lights have been seen floating around the battlements for many years and there are also reports of a phenomenon that manifests only as sound. This is the 'phantom drummer', a slow, rhythmic thumping that is only heard after dark.

Inexplicable drumming has also been reported from **Bolton Castle**, in Wensleydale. It is heard thumping up from the depths of the castle, where the stables, armoury and dungeons are situated. No story has been recorded to explain the sound. Two female phantoms have been seen at Bolton Castle. One is dressed in black, the other in white, and they appear to date from the Middle Ages. Mary, Queen of Scots was imprisoned here for six months, and she has been offered as a tentative identification for one of the apparitions. Bolton Castle was built in the 14th century and is open to the public. Among the many things of interest here is an old bed in

The striking ruins of Bolton Castle, another possible haunt of Mary, Queen of Scots.
Shutterstock/Marbury

which so many people have suffered nightmares that it has twice undergone an exorcism.

From fortresses to ruined religious houses. **Bolton Abbey** can be found east of Skipton in North Yorkshire (many miles south of the aforementioned Bolton Castle). The romantic ruins are just part of the attraction of this popular beauty spot. In addition there are the River Wharfe and miles of woodland walks to enjoy; the Priory Church; another medieval relic (Bardon Tower); and a steam railway. Bolton Abbey was actually a priory and its ghost is just what you might expect: that of a monk. He is dressed in the black habit of the Augustinian order and strolls from the oldest part of the ruins towards the Priory Church, which is intact and still

A spectral monk has been seen among the ruins of Bolton Abbey, near Skipton.
Shutterstock/Alastair Wallace

used as a place of worship today. The most dramatic sighting of this unassuming apparition took place when a rector saw what he took to be a real person being run over by a reversing van. He ran out in alarm, expecting to find someone crushed beneath the wheels, but of course there was no one there.

Even more celebrated is **Fountains Abbey**. Along with its neighbouring Georgian water gardens, the remains of Fountains Abbey are a World Heritage site and considered not only the most extensive but also one of Britain's most beautiful ecclesiastical ruins. The former Cistercian monastic house is now in the care of the National Trust. A ghostly choir has been heard by numerous witnesses in the vicinity of the Chapel of the Nine Altars, which was built in the 13th century. Nearby Fountains Hall (also National Trust) is haunted by a woman in a blue gown.

Kirkstall Abbey, on the outskirts of Leeds, was also a Cistercian monastery. Kirkstall is most famous for being owned by Archbishop Thomas Cranmer, who was given the lands by Henry VIII after the Dissolution of the Monasteries. Cranmer had been the king's right-hand man in creating the split with the Catholic Church. During 'Bloody' Mary I's brief reign, however, that same right hand was required to sign a confession of his contribution to the formation of Protestantism in England, a confession which led to him being burned at the stake despite a promise that he would not be punished. Cranmer is said to have plunged the hand that signed the confession into the rising flames to make sure it burned first.

A frightening spectre guards a hoard of treasure hidden somewhere below the ruins of Kirkstall Abbey. Shutterstock/Alastair Wallace

The ghost haunting Kirkstall Abbey's Gatehouse (now a museum) is not thought to be of Cranmer, however, but of an old abbot. He paces about the building as if deep in thought. The ruins themselves are haunted by a Barguest, one of those fearsome spectral dogs with blazing red eyes we met in Whitby and Sheffield. According to the legend, the spectre guards a hoard of gold hidden by a medieval treasurer of the Abbey.

GHOSTS IN THE OPEN

The four counties of Yorkshire are famous for their glorious countryside, in particular the Dales and the North York Moors, both of which are National Parks. Odd corners of these wide open spaces also harbour their ghosts.

Middleham Moor in the Yorkshire Dales, for example, is haunted by the ghost of a woman in the black gown and veil of deep mourning. The legend to explain her presence is that she made the mistake of stringing along two lovers. Eventually, she made up her mind which one she wanted but her plan to elope with him was discovered by the jilted suitor. In a jealous rage the spurned lover murdered the faithless woman on the moor. Evidence to substantiate the tale is claimed to have been uncovered when peat cutters found the skeleton of a woman to which clung the mouldering remnants of black clothing.

The sound of a woman weeping has been heard echoing eerily among the wide wastes of **Lockton Moor** at Saltergate, North Yorkshire. The origin of this mournful phenomenon is a mystery but some think it is the last desperate cries of a woman who became lost on the moor many years ago.

Yorkshire's best-known haunted moor is undoubtedly **Marston Moor**, North Yorkshire, where a decisive battle was fought on 2 July 1644, during the English Civil War. Prince Rupert of the Rhine led the Royalists and Oliver Cromwell the Parliamentarian forces. Cromwell suffered a wound to the neck but he was the clear victor. The Royalists were thoroughly routed: it is estimated more than four thousand were slaughtered by the Roundheads. A famous ghost sighting took place here in 1968 by tourists who had become lost and, without knowing it, found themselves driving on Atterwith Lane, the minor road which crosses the moor. They noticed 'half-a-dozen tramps' stumbling along a ditch beside the lane. Curious, they slowed down and saw then that the 'tramps' were wearing 17th-century costume. The tourists were just pondering on whether they were observing people engaged in a historical re-enactment when the 'tramps' vanished.

This was by no means the first sighting of phantom soldiers on Marston Moor. In November 1932 a driver who slowed down to let a bus pass near the now defunct Marston Moor railway station saw three men dressed as Cavaliers on the other side of the road. So did his passenger. The bus appeared to plough straight through them but they were nowhere afterwards to be seen. More recently, in 2006, local historian Christopher Linton had a spooky experience near the monument which commemorates the battle. In *Paranormal Magazine* he wrote: 'I heard what I can only describe as someone running on gravel, accompanied by heavy breathing and wheezing and the rattle of various accoutrements which a soldier may have worn during the battle.'

Mr Linton also mentions the ghost of a young woman who has been seen and also heard screaming near Wilstrop Wood on the edge of the former battlefield. Legend has it she was a girl who loyally opened a gate to help Royalist cavalrymen escape the carnage but who was then trampled to death by the Cavaliers' horses.

The unusual ghost which manifests on the cliffs near **Cloughton**, North Yorkshire, also relates to a tale of vengeance. According to legend, a young maid-servant who died while in service at Cloughton Hall in the 1830s blamed the attending physician on her death-bed for what she perceived as his incompetence. Whether he was incompetent or not cannot be ascertained but the doctor was certainly conscientious. Shortly after the maid's death, he was called out to an emergency during a spell of severe winter weather. It was a particularly bitter night but this didn't dissuade him from his duty. The parson accompanied him, just in case the patient proved to be beyond help and required spiritual comfort. As they were making their way through the snow, a large white hare suddenly leapt out of a hedge, startling the horses of the carriage, making them bolt. The parson was thrown clear and survived without serious injury but the doctor was killed. Ever since this fatal accident, the spirit of the vengeful maid-servant has haunted the scene in the form a spectral white hare.

A circular pit near **Flamborough** used to be pointed out as the place where a girl called Jenny committed suicide. It was believed that if a person made a circuit of the pit nine times,

Jenny's white-clad ghost would emerge. One foolish farmer who decided to put the tradition to the test was horrified when Jenny's furious ghost suddenly appeared and chased him all the way back to the village. She didn't quite catch him, but the savage spook took a bite out of his unfortunate horse's flank.

South of Whitby, yet another headless ghost haunts a place called **Fitz Steps** and also the bank of the River Esk as it passes under a disused Victorian railway viaduct. He appears to be dressed as a Royalist of the Civil War period. Old reports state that he carried his head beneath his arm, although more recent sightings suggest he may just be carrying his wide-brimmed feathered hat. On one memorable occasion in the early 1900s a pack of fox hounds spotted the apparition and, turning from their usual quarry, went in pursuit of him instead! This is very unusual behaviour for dogs, which normally back away from ghosts.

Many of Yorkshire's roads are haunted. In *The Ghost Hunter's Road Book*, author John Harries relates the story of 'Nance'. Nance was a young woman left with a baby by her highwayman lover near the end of the 18th century. A coachman spotted her shivering beside what is now the **A64** a few miles north of York, the child in her arms. He kindly pulled up and gave her a lift to the nearest inn. There, sadly, both Nance and her baby died. Two years later the same coachman was returning from the north and ran into thick fog. He could barely see the horses in front of him. Suddenly, the reins were twitched from his hands. Beside him sat the ghost of Nance, and she drove the horses at a gallop safely through the fog and into York. For many years later Nance's spirit haunted the road, always on the look-out to help

The old viaduct near Whitby beneath which a headless Cavalier has been seen.
Shutterstock/Paul Broadbent

travellers in trouble. She is even credited with preventing a hold-up, making the horses turn about just in time and pointing out the highwayman's accomplice in the coach.

The Great North Road, now the **A1**, has its tales of ghostly highwaymen. They tend to be linked to Dick Turpin, whose overnight ride from London to York has passed into legend, even though it was a work of pure fiction by Victorian novelist Harrison Ainsworth. Better substantiated is the ghost of highwayman Tom Hoggett, who has been seen on the A1 between Boroughbridge and Scotch Corner in North Yorkshire. 'The figure', writes John Harries, 'is of a man in a caped coat reaching to his ankles. It wears no hat. The ghost glides along the side of the road at great speed and periodically parts of the coat shine with a vague light as if being illuminated by a feeble lamp focused on it.'

80